SEATOWN AND EARLIER POEMS

CONOR O'CALLAGHAN

SEATOWN

AND EARLIER POEMS

Wake Forest University Press

Wake Forest University Press
This book is for sale only in North America.
Copyright © Conor O'Callaghan
First U.S. Edition published 2000. All rights reserved.
For permission, required to reproduce or broadcast
more than several lines, write to: Wake Forest University Press
Post Office Box number 7333, Winston-Salem, NC 27109
Printed in the United States of America by
Thomson-Shore. Text set in Stempel Garamond type
Library of Congress Catalogue Card 00-130159
ISBN 0-916390-91-8 (paperback)
ISBN 0-916390-92-6 (cloth)
The History of Rain and *Seatown*
were published in Ireland
by The Gallery Press
(Peter Fallon,
Editor)

Contents

For Eve

from *The History of Rain*

September

It must be a cliché to think, however brief,
that light on a wall and our voices
out in the open are the pieces
we shall look upon in retrospect as a life.

There is a danger of circumstance smothering
even the smallest talk. If a breeze
shakes another colour from the trees
we say a word like *withering*

without the slightest hint of irony.
After a season of fruitful conversation
and reflective pauses in the garden
we say we know what it means to be lonely.

Today the first moment of autumn tolls
like a refrain from the nineteen thirties.
The voices of friends and courtesies
are interrupted by thunder and the radio crackles.

We shall remember it as the impending doom
and use this afternoon as an example of decay
when there is nothing left for us to say
and September has outstayed its welcome.

Today our clothes will be spoiled by rain.
We shall drag from the lawn the chairs and table
that all summer made us comfortable.
Though all of that remains to be seen.

The Last Cage House in Drogheda

Made bi Nicholas Bathe in the ieare
of our lord 1570 bi hiv Mor carpenter

Maybe a final order from the sheriff was sent
after the neighbours complained it was an eyesore
and, because the oak had been stolen from Mellifont,
claimed that some god had settled an old score
when the floorboards smelt and the beams were rotten.
But who lived there, and where they went, is forgotten.

All that survives is an unpeopled picture
with the first owner's inscription. It traps
in pencil on a page of mist the architecture
of a crumbling age and someone's understandable hopes
that the place where so many people once lived
would, despite the weather, be somehow saved.

Maybe the heir in a family of settlers
left instructions for the lot to be pulled down
after he returned to a different cold in Chester.
Or a pail that caught two centuries of rain
was thrown away, and with it a clatter
of tenants stepped out to freedom and squalor.

The only certainty is that one morning in Drogheda
in 1825 an amateur draughtsman turned up early,
and for half a day passers-by stopped and saw
the corner of Shop St. and Laurence St. differently.
Then tea-chests filled with earthenware and spoons
were stacked onto the cobbles in the late afternoon.

And someone alone upstairs probably recognised
history being listened to from a particular angle
for the last time, while boys whistling outside
could see no meaning in the single
martin rising from the thatch, or yellow bars
on the floor and worktop that were just wiped bare.

Say someone who had shared one room with her husband
and with her husband's friend and his nephew;
who wondered if anything that had been left behind
could be used again, and thought how the years flew;
who, with the final call, put a spray of harebells
in a jam jar on the ledge, to be gathered in the rubble.

The Swimming Pool

The swimming pool on the headland shuts in October,
when the gate dwindles and the lifeguard believes
it's pointless to carry on netting the water
littered with the autumnal débris of Coke cans and leaves.

I break in through the back out of season
and watch it rustle on the surface more than usual,
as if it's about to return to the surf and rain
on the far side of the turquoise wall.

Sometimes a gale or an occasional storm
shatters across the rocks, only to find
the end is never clear and the wall holds firm
despite the predictions of graffiti and the wind.

Which now and then is what makes me wander
out on a limb before another year is closed,
to reflect on the edges of a shape and to ponder
scraps of waves like phrases that are left unused.

Everything is as it was when the railed doors
were locked. Now the stile only gives
to south-westerlies that freckle the diving board
and the concrete seats. Everything and nothing moves.

The edges of the swimming pool are the last
lines visible when shapelessness comes
with evening like a fine spray and the aftertaste
of chlorine lingers from the changing rooms.

I write my name and the date with a stone,
and make it scatter gulls that disappear
into the air, and resolve once again
to learn to swim in the new year.

A tourist notice gives the distance back to town.
I say 'Will closing time continue until summer?'
to test my voice out loud across the deep end,
then leave the way I came without an answer.

Outside all of this endures a mess
of squalls and winter on the corrugated strand
where someone who couldn't care less
walks towards the torn sky and England.

In summer shapes appear more precise.
The colours of the swimming pool
are exact again, and are cemented as one place.
The sun is hardly broken, and days swell.

Mengele's House

It was considered
the finest in its street
on the outskirts of Buenos Aires.
Splashing and screams were heard
during the long July heat
in adjacent gardens.

Nobody has lived there
since the last family fled.
Now and then a researcher comes,
or a would-be buyer
armed with rosary beads
noses around the bedrooms.

Since all the glass
was kicked from a window
by legless students,
the lambency of trees
is free to come and go
in the gutted kitchen.

Out the back are piles
of twigs and compost,
a seventies lawnmower
and aquamarine tiles,
exactly as they were left
by the last owner,

who talked about himself a lot,
chatting across the fence,
but never had the neighbours
past his gate,
and never even once
darkened their doors.

In the neighbourhood
he's remembered still.
He was the old misery
who had strange kids,
a swimming pool,
and a history.

Watching Clouds

Each time the force of cloud weathers the sky
we attempt to emulate their purpose in fire.

> Or in pulling back the window to mute the wind
> notice earlier moons brightened by a shoal of coral.

Once we left the house for the longest space
that we could find between fast clouds and midday.

> For several hours we were divided by an emerald storm
> that followed and caught us from the nearest horizon.

It separated against our arms and against our clothes.
In the end we were welcomed up to the outskirts of town.

> Now, in December, dawns stand behind pylons
> and enamel clouds. Afternoons clear to the headland

littered with fallen shells to watch a blue fleet
blown across the edges of the hemisphere.

> Two miles away we notice the doors swell and jar,
> or work on in the yard speckled by fine rain.

On Re-entering the Lavender City

On re-entering the lavender city
on a warm Christmas, I am struck
by the absence of noise. Today only
the turrets and flags remain; they break
into inaudible colour and the sky
broods on the streets where I walk.

In your house we talk again
of the Wedgwood pieces,
matching them to the afternoon.
We talk of how each design successfully
depicts a Victorian
world that would preserve every movement

as the eternal flurry into stillness;
of delft traders, disused ox-carts,
merchant ships, tea clippers.
On a day of heavy pigments,
almost completely without people,
except for two who turn from the port

and begin up even steps
to where a pattern of deserted streets
is the aftermath of some great event.
We talk of how something is lost
when we realise what we protect;
how the mountains of the world are vast

and how the city wall
is just a lilac flame,
a garland of forget-me-nots and blue roses.
We agree a storm
is necessary within that stillness
for the flags and the wind to be the same.

Although we like the way everything
of then and now is constant
in a one-hundred-year old jug:
the blown horizon, the water's end;
the way the place of blue and white things
and its finished sounds,

and their absence, all stay intact;
or returning to your house, how I find
the same instants of rest
still unbroken, while outside
a lavender sky has cracked
the evening with thin fire.

The Dream of Edward Elgar

There's a story the composer
used to tell. About weeks
in the middle of a hard winter
when insomnia, silence, and sickness
were the only prayers he could hear.
And about the evening he returned to work

until *The Dream of Gerontius* was complete,
after hearing voices outside,
and, in a downpour of sleet,
helping a neighbour bind
a blizzard of sheep
away from darkness and the road.

In a letter to a friend
some years later, he seemed
moved by the ease of it all,
by the passing sounds and the ease
with which each note fell,
almost taken to be real.

He said he thought the simple
movement was the same
as that from night-blindness to understanding shapes.
As each time, finished in the drawing-room,
he would blow against a lamp
and find himself blindfolded in a pallid gloom.

Until the last shapes of his age
separated, and night snowed
against the mirror, the cream drapes,
the notepaper, the piano,
the lampshade,
the mantelpiece, the bay window.

Home

Your family home is gone. On open ground I stand and say:
I am standing in the front room, in the hallway,
in the kitchen. I am standing at the foot of the stairs . . .
to continue the pretense of knowing where everything once was.

Everything now is exaggerated by an evening late in June,
the last minutes of childhood. You close the curtains
of your bedroom. For a short while you listen to the ancient
sound of your father's car running at the gate.

A Pear Tree at Knowth, Planted 1880

When he came back from the world with shells
and coloured cloth, Mr Thompson planted a pear tree
for the birth of his only daughter.
Now she is eighteen, his stories remain
in a world of Saturdays alone, her uncle
returning with news of trouble farther down the country,
the same bleak polonaise crackling at tea.
On the hill at Knowth she shows her brother
the horizons of the earth. Before spots of thunder
arrive from the midlands, and they run
for the house, their baskets forgotten,
to shelter from the falling of the imminent century.

Song

I built my house the wrong way round
with the outside in and the inside out.
I have been under the weather ever since,
hoping the world will make inverted sense.

The home of my dreams no longer seems likely
now the process of decay has started so quickly.
The carpet and curtains, though still quite new,
are perpetually soggy with berries and dew.

The bath and toilet can be seen from the gate,
in the upstairs bedrooms sparrows mate,
a chair from the lounge lies toppled on the lawn,
the floral wallpaper peels in the sun.

The formica is warped on the kitchen press
where a family of swallows has made its nest.
The windows are moulding, their frames are rotten,
the calendar is torn, the radio broken.

I built my house the wrong way round
and now the world seems inside out.
I convince myself that everything's clearer
when the heat goes in and the days cloud over.

Then I shelter from sudden squalls
in the room at the centre with pebble-dashed walls
and a ceiling of slates turned in from the sky
to a darkened space where no birds fly.

Poachers

The whole island
agrees they should be
ashamed of themselves,
whoever they are.

On the late walk
home, I pause
at the top of the road
and make out

between waves
the whispers
of poachers
in a boat

in the stars,
their unwise
laughter that
can't be helped.

The Ocean

We wanted to go to the ocean,
to undress and make love,
so drove across the hottest afternoon
on record, with the sun roof

wide open, to where you were sure
would be a deserted cove.
But found, miles from anywhere,
that it wasn't entirely unheard of.

We agreed to take the plunge
as far from the crowd as possible.
We dared each other to change
without once using a towel.

At one point we just lay
at the edge of the surf in togs
and tried to get carried away.
It was useless. Too many dogs,

and fathers in snorkel and flippers,
and kids playing football,
and scorched day-trippers
watching from *The Blue Yonder Hotel.*

In the end we drove home
the same evening, and arrived late
to find the kitchen and living-room
had absorbed the city's heat.

I'd say we both remember this
when something in the small hours gives,
or when a train behind the house
passes like a handful of waves.

The Swimming Pool

This is the inland silence that allows
no sounds to enter. It is also dawn.

The rockery is black with the sun behind.
Outside, the world has yet to start.

The step I take from the edge into the shallows
makes no ripples on the white day that follows.

A Large Diver

— David Hockney, 1978

The twenty-seventh and last essay
on water and light

on the human figure.
Gregory has just dived

from a July day in upstate
New York and splashed

the perception of heat as tiles
and corners and transparent shadows.

The grass will only be still,
the gravel unblemished,

for as long as he can hold his breath.
When work re-starts in another garden

and cars on the new freeway
are heard a mile from here

this second will be scattered
by ripples like gulls

and by a restlessness to break out
from paper pools, and move on.

Pigeons

Busty never asked me why I came around.
Twice a week we cycled to the farthest hill
to shake his pigeons from a *Marietta* box, knowing
they'd be back before us in half-light on the wall.

He was with my father, on short-term hire.
I invented messages to go and watch sheet metal
being splintered to gold. The others laughed
behind his back because he hardly spoke at all.

Then the welders were let go, and he was gone.
On the first evening of the holidays
I found his yard in tatters, the loft on its side,
the wire spattered with feathers, white and grey.

I kept trying the bell, and listened to it ring
in the hall until night built behind the town.
There was no answer. My mother told me
to sit in the front room and calm down.

He spoke its name each time he threw a pigeon
in the air and saw it broke from the initial stutter.
I felt a small heart in my palm for days after,
and my father's taunt: 'I told you he wasn't all there.'

The story goes . . . he packed his bags
and sat out all night; he was heard at dawn,
shouting and shouting; the whole of Dundalk
woke to clouds flyblown with homing pigeons.

River at Night

for Vona

We do this at least once a year.
The midges, the cow parsley, the stagnant air

are signposts to the only deep enough pool
after weeks have dried the current to a trickle.

After too much heat, and too much cider,
the night seems forever and the water inviting.

We have walked for miles into unfenced land
where the hum of the distant town is drowned,

and find again that the core of summer
is cold against our sun-burned shoulders.

There's no special way of deciding who goes first.
It just happens that my jeans and tee-shirt

have been left on parched, hoof-marked earth
where a cigarette ripens closer to your mouth.

On the other bank, an orchard and the sky's
expanse spread out like a field of fireflies.

No birdsong, nothing swaying in the high grass,
and little that ties us to what we recognise.

The silence is only disturbed by your voice
saying it can't possibly be so easy,

the planets blossoming. Only the remote throng
of cars at closing time asks if this is wrong.

To forget ourselves and a world more sober.
To forget that the slow persistence of the river

among black horses, black ragwort, black crab-apple trees
is just the brief eternity between two boundaries.

That when we walk this way in a different year
the same sense of longing will still be here.

On the surface of the universe my splashing
and your laughter scarcely make an impression.

After the silence has resumed you say that at some
point we should think of turning back. Come.

For now the night is shining on your arms.
Imagine that we've shaken off the sun and its harness.

Take off your bracelet and your black dress,
and stretch out across the confluence of two days

to where I am, floating in darkness.

Different Sunflowers

Versions of a poem by Montale

1

I have been given a sunflower
that I have placed in singed ground
in a garden in the south, where the colours
of the bay and the air are shadowed by its moods.

Now what I say is only difficult
if it becomes easily said.
When I walk to the end of a room
my face and arms move into light and sound.

I have been given a shoot
that I am told will open to the noon vapours.
I have been given a sunflower
and its illusions of light.

2

I wanted to give you a sunflower
to plant in the white earth of your garden
near the coast, to turn its frown
to the reflected blues of sea and air,

I wanted you to know the complexity
of everything that seems straightforward,
that to disappear is to be lucky
like figures streaming into shade and sound.

I wanted you to have the seed of light
where living is ignored as air.
I wanted to give you a sunflower
distracted by that light.

3

Bring to my home a sunflower
so that I can plant it in soil
bittered by the sea wind, and show its yellow
face to the opposing blues of sky and water.

Eventually the obscure thing
faces back towards clarity,
and the warm limbs of shade and song
are merged into accidents of movement.

Bring me the plant of life
dispersing the mists of summer.
Bring to my home a sunflower
deranged by the sunlight.

Postcard

I've spent the last week inside,
lounging around, making a list
of all that's mine and all that's lost.
Now there's little else for me to add.

In three days I leave for good.
Everyone else keeps saying
how great it would be if I could
choose words for leaving and staying,

and manage to capture my feelings
with something not too vague or unkind.
So I've written some rhetorical questions,
said the weather's bad and nothing's changed.

I'm tired of that. Today's warm and bright.
I'm writing this lying on my parents' bed,
the blinds drawn, with daylight
between myself and the rest of the world.

Silver Birch

Here, in time, the words for trees will
be darkness's other names (lime, ash, evergreen)
and will alter what happens. Today I read
the pages where a generation falls still.

In my book the plain of Birkenau
opens into the surrounding fields
of silver birch that once sealed
it within its name . . . *from the German* . . .

The branches of the past rumble in the wind.
Some parents tell their children to go on
listening to the trees before they are gone,
that each leaf is a minute turning to the ground.

I read of the gypsy encampment near their home
and the day in October when it is lit with war.
I read of those who pass through there
for years to come, remembering their freedom.

The day is gone. My longest memory of trees
is the one in which I walk across a road
to where silver birch leaves are darkened on one side.
The shadows from a story will survive like this.

Seatown

Seatown

Sanctuary of sorts for the herons all day yesterday
waiting for the estuary to drain and this evening
for two lights queuing like crystal at the top of the bay.

Last straw for the panel beaters only just closed down
and the dole office next to the barracks and the gold
of beer spilled on the pavements of Saturday afternoon.

Home from home for the likes of us and foreign boats
and groups with oilskins and unheard-of currencies
in search of common ground and teenage prostitutes.

Reclaimed ward of bins left out a week and dogs in heat
and the fragrance of salt and sewage that bleeds
into our garden from the neap-tide of an August night.

Poor man's Latin Quarter of stevedores and an early house
and three huge silos swamped by the small hours
and the buzz of joyriders quite close on the bypass.

Time of life to settle for making a fist of love
and glimpsing new dawns and being caught again
and waking in waves with all the sheets kicked off.

Point of no return for the cattle feed on the wharves
and the old shoreline and the windmill without sails
and time that keeps for no one, least of all ourselves.

May its name be said for as long as it could matter.
Or, failing that, for as long as it takes the pilot
to negotiate the eight kilometres from this to open water.

Landscape with Canal

So this, the means to an end, is chosen
as the landscape of a private fiction
where the tracks you make are all-too-well-known.
Though this time, since whatever will happen
will happen most likely in the open,
you set it in a derelict autumn
when all its symbolic fruit has fallen.
The action is yours alone to govern.
As long as you make the silence broken
by the presence on the bank of someone
that's both anticipated and sudden.
As long as you don't forget to mention
that the voice at once without and your own
is the one that leaves the rest unspoken
and between the past and town has taken
the long way around a simple question.

Say, if you wish, your surrogate father
who charmed the birds in a yard of feathers.
Or say the shade of the young schoolmaster
who sometime during your last free summer
was dumped by his girl for something better
and found with a shotgun two days later
on a disused farm before the border.
The choice is yours — it will scarcely matter.
There'll be in the distance a curfew hour
knelled across the not-so-familiar.
Walking back the shortcut none the wiser
through the mill and the gates of the manor
there must always be some faceless other
on the towpath by the slick of water
who'll call in the murk ahead, 'Who goes there?'
and call once more when you don't quite answer.

The Swimming Pool

It goes under, the cursor, whenever I place my finger
on the space bar and hold it like this for a minute.
The blue screen shimmers the way a pool's sunlit
floor moves after the splash of a lone swimmer.

As long as this minute lasts, the season is somewhere
between July and dawn: the soundless underwater
of sandals left out overnight and garden furniture,
that will end, but could just as easily go on forever.

I could be forgiven for forgetting that it was ever there.
The pool is only still again when I take away my finger.
Unthinking, and unable to hold its breath any longer,
as much as two pages further, it comes up for air.

Progging

Once. To a garden in drizzle
and the orchard of a half-crippled
stretcher-bearer in the Order of Malta
who sat out every second Sunday at the football.
There on the scud from school
and back on the track behind the hospital
with a jumperful
of cookers and Cox's Pippins no bigger than marbles.

The word got to the old man
by the five o'clock buzzer.
His sulk at tea, a half-hour at sea
alone in the good room,
and a half-baked sermon
about my new sweater and poor mother
was about the closest he ever came
to raising his hand to me.

So much for the first blossom and the last.
So much for the darkening past
and the usual attempts
to suggest knowledge (in the erotic sense).
So much for any chance
to behold once more the innocence
of Eden,
beside the lesson taught and night all of a sudden.

In the beginning was the word,
after that the original thrill.
Just saying it since then
has called for the sequence of a squandered
adolescence that ends
at me, with two syllables
on my hands,
being asked to explain myself. Never again.

The Good Room

Tumblers dusted down every once in a blue moon
and coats in the hall and silver asleep in the drawer
and the brass fireguard last thing and the good sense
   never to outstay a welcome.

That and holidays locked away and the good china sets
and faded heat and a carriage clock converted to quartz
and twice a year the footless newly-weds in the music-box
   waltzing to 'The Isle of Capri'.

Or pine needles on the mat after January is unwrapped
and bits of Dresden and a hemisphere shaken to blizzards
and cut-glass sprinkled with the tinsel of cars on the street
   and the shutting door. Goodnight.

The good room waits through it all — through darkness
and the month of Sundays saved this long on the shelf
in the wishful belief that a reason in the long run
   will be good enough to call.

The Gate Lodge

The inkpot at the entrance to a midlands estate
that once housed a herdsman and a herdsman's family,

complete with leaded astragals in the windows at the front,
a page of pointers from a friend of a friend,

a lean-to at the back strewn with flies
and fishing rods, a mangle still in use,

and a three month lease about to close
on the closest thing to a drought in living memory.

❧

The great house itself — wingless, Palladian,
levelled in the Civil War to the state we left it in.

We made for it a past tense of terraces at dusk,
to forget the present reign of nettles and hearsay.

We even had the 7th Marquis of Something-or-Other
pay for the stone at the crossroads to a dozen pals

who bowed their hats when their betters were passing
and marched to Passchendaele for much the same reason.

❧

A landscape littered with antiquated machinery
that gradually gave rise to an antiquated vocabulary:

like the coinbox halfway to *The Shepherd's Rest*
swallowing nothing except pennies and florins;

threshers and rusting breadvans waist deep
all day long in swathes of motionless heat;

the turquoise Hillman Hunter lying belly-up
at the back door, in rosehip and wayfarer's friend.

One afternoon, for something to do as much as anything,
we fucked on the mattress on the boards upstairs,

and fell asleep, and woke there stuck to each other
and to someone else's cast-off flannel sheets.

How long had elapsed? Cattle out at the gate
were drifting past in a haze of dust and time.

The kitchen radio was serving muffled applause for tea
on the fourth day at Lord's, or for another century.

All history now. Teenagers wailing on the bridge
or wading after each other's shadows

through a meadow of long neglected words;
and goldfinches diving at sunset from nowhere

to a pool of reflected branches; and at night
broad-leafs without half-lit by the anglepoise within;

and ever July's ache to trek at dawn
to the dried river and drink the oncoming air.

Doubtless somewhere between two market towns
we'll stumble again upon that moment and that road.

Leaving a locked car for ten minutes or so,
we'll stand there forgetting what we ever saw

in an age since by-passed by the county planners.
The gate will have been sold and the lodge let go.

Doubtless somewhere down the line we'll stumble
upon that wishful moment and that latening road.

None of which explains exactly why the summer gave.
Except that after frogs were swept around the lino,

and the one tape of lute-music turned over and over,
and two hundred and twelve games of *Memory* later,

the pastoral life began to seem at best like
a running joke, at worst a slamming door.

None of which explains how August's empty threats
became, in retrospect, our days of thunder.

Tonight it's just from something left unsaid,
sitting late, across our own kitchen table.

As if even yet, at several sensible removes,
our every pause is thrown by an otherwhere

where time is dust and droves of moths like angels
are clipping a yard-light's autumnal halo.

We can all but hear them, lit in darkness there
(if dark it is by now, if lit they are).

Sublet

Within their rented lives I am the gate at all hours,
footsteps on the stairs that might wake their child.
I am a spare set of clothes in the box-room wardrobe,
a misremembered name, the cistern's muffled hum,
a sliver across the landing that widens and shuts over.
I am a temporary measure until things pick up,
a cousin from the west if the landlord asks,
a couple of used notes in advance on the telly
that come as a godsend in the middle of the month.
I am a wafer-thin book that was left by mistake
one weekend on the table, the latest running joke
with her sister, his mother, a reason to whisper.
I am a strange alarm clock, the lukewarm kettle,
a cup no one else uses upside-down by the sink,
the missing inch of milk, a change of plan in red ink
on the back of a napkin. I am a half-minute lull
as the house holds its breath, a rustle in the hall,
the front door slamming onto mid-morning rain.

There's No One Here at the Moment

It happens once, in his absence.
The bright hall rings, rings and, mid-ring,
clicks back over into silence.

It leaves two isolated sighs,
hers, momentarily frozen
before an ocean of blank space

that by nightfall he'll come across
and save against the backdrop of
a Friday evening office;

give up on; rewind to and play
more times than make sense; tomorrow,
or the day after, wipe away.

Johnny

Made from Glasgow a fatherless trip
with two small sisters, this clock in his lap.

Was sure to have his mother's words straight:
'We won't go back to Tullyard tonight.'

Thought nothing of rambling twelve miles away
to listen to Madame Markievicz in her heyday.

Heard his brother being taken by the Tans
the morning after a night at a dance.

Tutored his uncle's whiskey with water
while the heavens teemed with German bombers.

Inherited three rooms, a dishevelled chaise longue,
a handbag of photos, a phone no one rang.

Never married nor ever really came close
though called on a friend of the family, twice.

Always fretted when we arrived in the car
and were still at the table with darkness near.

Threatened to follow us to Swanns Cross and back
with supper and a bottle of tea in a sock.

Made a fist of the world by touch and sound
when he couldn't see past his nose in the end.

Somewhere yet in his own perfect memory
two churns left at the well for the creamery,

the dog he was wild about but had to drown,
the polythene glasshouse, the Newbliss train.

When did he start as a hand for Lord Guthrie?
August 3rd, 1923.

What does a corncrake sound like really?
Like nothing as much as an evening in July.

Blood

1

Freddie, my mother's mother's brother:
his only souvenir of a life at sea
a cuckoo clock from land-locked Switzerland
that we begged him to sway beneath
with a stick in his hand until midnight
had struck at least six or seven times.

He said the waves were in our blood
or something as daft I took literally.
Still, even after the briefest crossing,
I will lie in a strange bed on my back
and feel rows upon rows of cold water
folding over white at first, then black.

2

Now one cousin alone shoulders
the weight of knowing he's the last
in the family line to go down that road,
along with the memory of his new wife
and the light of their house cut off
between Land's End and Penzance.

Immediately after his own da's wake
he went out again, to clear his head.
The month that he was gone, trawling
for plaice on Biscay and Finisterre,
became too much. She was lying there
for at least four days when he found her.

3

A meal to mark my twenty-ninth.
About closing time, as the last diners
gather at the bar for *Match of the Day*,
we totter back into the seafront's murk,
believing the cab that a waiter called
is bound to roll along at any moment.

No. Nor is the sea anywhere in sight.
We can hear it though, if scarcely at first,
miles off, like a generator which keeps
one of those tundral outposts ticking over:
numb, echoic. By the time I hold
the cab door open, it is deafening.

Swanns Cross

for my mother, Joan McCabe

No landmarks, no legends, and certainly no swans.
Nothing to speak of besides a bridge, a post office,
a fuchsia door to a garden. Not even the token sense
that roads diverging are symbolic of a moral choice.

It's just that my grandfather on my mother's side
was once recognised being herded through Swanns Cross
and I got stuck there decades later, thumbing a ride
between outposts along the edge of the wilderness.

That's about it. I admit, it's not much of a story.
Not even with the sub-plot in which his own mother
stepped two townlands to help at a difficult delivery
and, returning with an apron of eggs for her bother,

saw a neighbour running to meet her with the news.
Since that day his future and its shadow have gone
their separate ways. Her memory has outlived its use.
And I, needless to say, have been happy to let on

that the past's simplicity is somewhere inviolable
like the quietness of a room before word comes:
lamplight flecking the pattern of an atlas on the table,
a glass, a penknife, a copybook darned with sums.

Sunday Drinking

No. Not the epiphanies
stumbled upon like
sunlit winter seas.

Not the peninsula
in brightness, nor stepping
into darkness, nicely.

Nothing falls in place
for swearing 'Never again'.
Nothing important changes.

For a couple of hours
and languid rounds,
in easy chairs

between the window
and the pool table,
with a view

across the lough's
noiseless turmoil,
even the caravan parks

of Cranfield and Greencastle
seem remote
and beautiful.

Then the inevitable
tumbles in from nowhere
while the TV mumbles

News for the Deaf.
The day is suddenly
a shadow of itself,

the wall clock
mislays the last
bright hour gone back,

and all the boys and girls,
miles out of their way,
stir themselves

from the heat
of a log fire
that will plug out.

From here on in
only a rim of lights
defining the town,

the headache
of cold rooms bleached
from habitual black.

No stars showing through.
No porch-light's
expectant glow.

No work further on.
No voices waiting
on the answering machine.

Nothing to watch, or do,
or burn, or eat.
Nothing to look forward to.

No promise of snow
or anything so simple
as a better tomorrow.

Nothing to hope for
anymore except
weekends of more

of much the same. No.

In the Neighbourhood

The humidity these nights is second to none.
Sleep has become a blank cheque
punctuated by cars from the apartment blocks
and the worry that honeysuckle on its trellis
out our back is killing everything else there
and the memory of the telly's missing zapper.

Lately, across the way, Number 89
is out on short-term lease
to a handful of greasy little pricks
who bury the parenthetic
no-man's-land that Saturdays share
with Sundays under thrash-metal and 'Deutschland über

Alles' sung in alternating strains past sunrise
with 'Glory, Glory Man. Utd.' in the afternoon,
as the heat soars up, I take a raincheck
on Schopenhauer
in an attempt to follow one of the earlier
classic episodes of *Twin Peaks*.

By six the *Golden Gate's* fragrance of sweet and sour
with pineapple chunks
has wafted across an acre of neon
to our kitchen table (where my darling wife, I realise,
has just declared, 'If I see another
fucking sestina, I'll scream' — she picks

her moments). And admittedly I have been known
to play the concerned citizen with an older
couple three doors over, between a shower
and dusk's welcome release.
This evening it's Number 50's Pekinese
and the shit it leaves on the path like bits of chalk.

We are occupying the space in which, from now on,
their prodigal son parks.
They have had their fair share
of knocks. I am elsewhere,
thinking of the two-day-old chick
my own son and daughter drowned in tomato relish.

She says there are no rules anymore. And no, I assure her,
my hands in my pockets and my tongue down in
the neighbourhood of my cheek. No, I don't get it either.

She Waits for News . . .

by the glimmer of an eight-band Grundig wireless.
The kitchen lately is occupied with thoughts
of places that will never belong to her.
She flits over Belgrade, Athlone, Munich,
and makes the whole continent mumble and waltz.
She sits and waits past midnight and tiredness
for word to fall between forecasts for snow.
The teacup stops steaming. The clock's tick
unwinds into silence. I don't understand why
she forsakes our bed to be the first to hear
the story break; or how, in the end, she can cry
for states and suffering she will never know.

Pitch & Putt

Its is the realm of men
and boys joined in boredom,
the way of life that sees
one day on a par
with the next and school breaks
dragged out too long.

Theirs is the hour killed slowly,
the turn for home
in diminishing threes and twos,
the provisional etiquette
of shared tees,
conceded defeat.

Theirs the loose end,
the nationality of ships
in the absence
of shop to talk,
the freedom to be hopeless
and still come back.

Theirs the blather
of the last twoball
accepting flukes
for what they are,
the greenkeeper collecting flags
and shadows in their wake.

Ships

I am given to mistaking
the rumble of cranes around dawn
for dry shapeless thunder at sea,
to going weeks on end without sleep.

❧

Her father tended the pile light
like an allotment of lettuce,
too wordless in times and levels
to care, too fogbound to notice.

❧

I've come around to thinking ships
are the only visible bridge
between the earth's darkened centre
and its sunlit peripheries.

❧

Just once, I called her bluff between
the grain stores and two waves of heat.
Days after, on a rush-hour train,
her salt was still on my fingers.

❧

Lately I find I can lie here
listing their grey ports in my head —
Hull and Bergen and Bilbao
and Riga — without drifting off.

❧

I have taken it all on board:
her distance and her brother's death
and her big wedding to a prick
of a stevedore from abroad.

Behind the chimney smoke at eight
and the park and pitch & putt flags
and the bypass, a coal freighter's
constellation edges away.

Just once, let me be her husband,
climbing in behind her after
a twelve-hour shift, stirring her with
sweet nothings in a foreign tongue.

The Bypass

There are no ships in the
                    docks. It has been raining.
It falls to us like this with each successive week,
the vague sense of being cut adrift or drowning
that sleeplessness accentuates.
                              Then a while back
it dawned on me that we
                    had made our home on land
that is reclaimed. Ever since I have been at sea.
They have cut a bypass over the Lower End,
from the halting sites to
                    the bird sanctuary.
It is the latest in
              a long stream of removes
from the outside world. It is finished. It crosses
Seatown within earshot of here in even waves
between the tool hire yard
                    and the early houses.
It has given our lives
                    an edge. It's out there now,
going through the motions of distance and darkness,
matter-of-fact, an orchard ripening yellow,
making time and deadlines
                    and midsummer starless,
a latter-day silk route
                    murmuring with fireflies,
piling itself up at traffic lights, pointillist,
then shifting through its gears, beautiful and tireless,
a droning scarcely
                    audible though always just,
like moths at the window
                    or next door's radio
left running for months, a heavy relentless hum
that quickens past eight and we turn in and wake to,

not once diminishing
                        or losing momentum,
whether hauliers in
                        articulated trucks
or joyriders at speed or motorbikes in swarms
or sirens ebbing on the old shore like tidemarks
or Saturday's tail-back
                        exhaling its sweet fumes,
a necklace lying away
                        out on the marshes
and the mile of disused industrial estates,
linking cities, migrant, a river that washes
its own hands of silence,
                        that dusk accelerates,
that almost dries to a
                        standstill if never quite,
day and night and day and night, not once letting up,
half-dreamt, a buzz constantly in my head of late
and even yet as I
                        write. It will never stop.

Seatown

Short-term investment prolonged with every shrunken day
and drizzle that threatens to blow over though seldom does
and the glitter of headlights all morning on the motorway.

Outpost of a thousand chimneys and pubs shut early midweek
and snooker halls half empty and property prices frozen
and a smattering of traffic with the Chinese and the dog track.

Stop-gap to the constant warbling of an alarm streets from here
and our birdtable flattened and the saying about Saturday's flitting
that's meant as a harmless joke but remembered as something more.

Doldrums of the sea itself flooding fields almost up
to the racecourse one minute and then abstract and removed
the next like the untelevised rounds of the FA Cup.

Season of a set day utterly dead and the half-hearted euphoria
of the year seen off with a handful of neighbours' doors
and the stammering of a foghorn from as far away as Estonia.

Swansong to a blizzard of stars and snow-clouds from the brewery
and bits of coal like windfalls scattered on the road
and the first blanket that sticks the very last thing in February.

Exile self-imposed in the hope of belonging if only once
and change that only happens the moment you don't want it to
and a hangover from the hour gone forward that drags for months.

May the length it takes to leave go some distance to explain
a sense of marking time and that gradual ache inside, despite
a pile of boxes undiminished in the hall, which says, 'I could go on.'

For the Road

Again, between pausing for breath and going on, resumes
the study of the figure by itself on a remote dust-path.
Again the close sky and the point past which,
through fuchsia and pylons, one way or another comes.

Comes the day like today when it's dry enough for you
to sit in the heavy air. When this familiar face
calls by and describes again for hours in your place
the same old plans that you drink one more time to.

To the privilege of choosing either to up and go
or not, as the case may be. To the countries of cloud
that are visible from your gate, and the white road
between that each longer evening takes a shine to.

To the afternoons such as these that refuse to rain.
To the furniture in your orchard, your open book,
and your voice making fun of yours truly, whose like
keeps threatening never to be seen this way again.

Nobody You'd Know

Light-headed; wearing the last week in May
like a new dress for no real occasion;
staying on late; careless; thinking forwards
as though the verb *to love* has no past tense;
barely back just as the city rises,
the kitchen lamp turned on; lying by me;
hot; post-coital; smelling of roses;
unchanged; breathing too easily for words.
Miles away since; haunted by a slow march
on long wave; kept awake now by the lost
earring of a special pair and mail trains
all night behind the flat; tired chasing;
taken these days for granted, or at least
given to silences that say as much.

Anon

What's my name? What am I?
Call it an old-fashioned riddle,
a snapshot of the perfect family
with a blind spot in the middle.

A schooling in remedial care
that became a brilliant adolescence.
A hometown twinned with somewhere
in one of the grimmer parts of France.

A mother sporadically given to tears,
a career in the civil service,
a father weeks on end upstairs
suffering with his nerves.

A bigger brother, slightly thick,
by now should be in his forties.
He once got to the edge of Munich
on the strength of the hurdy-gurdies.

His passport and his example,
and a penchant for the cold,
made it seem vaguely simple
to give up the lights of old

for two years covering tracks
across a continental wilderness
of hotels and three-star sex,
and two since that amount of this.

Four languages, a duplex flat,
a position of a certain standing,
seven colleagues in a similar boat
and an office spirit demanding

that we all have fun together.
Seven affected levels of smiling
to disguise a complete and utter
contempt for ten-pin bowling.

One eighth of a second-hand yacht
bought imagining the horizon
that would, as like not,
bring me finally into my own.

An empty garage, nine pairs of shoes,
more flings than anyone can count,
and a balcony with a southward view
that's nothing to write home about.

A girlfriend who has tiny breasts
and a quiet way with children,
whose restlessness is expressed
by her need for a happy ending.

She teaches weekdays in the hills,
comes on my couch on Friday night
between the news and late film,
and leaves on Monday in a suit.

Love is neither here nor there.
We just have our moments.
She expects no one with her
for New Year at her parents'.

Apart from her a lovely sense
of being isolated and somehow clean
when the festive wishes of friends
are wiped off the answering machine,

and most of the TV stations
have long since been snowbound,
and one of the bathroom curtains
is moved by the indifferent wind.

That and dreams about drowning
or running head-on into gales,
that only come after returning
from a night alone on the tiles.

But no interest when she cries,
and no ambitions for the past.
No two ways, no ties,
no cheques, no questions asked.

Nor resolutions either way
to go or leave things the same,
throw all again or stay.
What am I? What's my name?

East

I know it's not playing Gaelic, it's simply not good enough,
to dismiss as someone else's all that elemental Atlantic guff.
And to suggest everything's foreign beyond the proverbial pale
would amount to a classic case of hitting the head on the nail.

But give me a dreary eastern town that isn't vaguely romantic,
where moon and stars are lost in the lights of the greyhound track
and cheering comes to nothing and a flurry of misplaced bets
blanketing the stands at dawn is about as spiritual as it gets.

Where back-to-back estates are peppered with satellite discs
and the sign of the *Sunrise Takeaway* doesn't flick on until six
and billows from the brewery leave a February night for dead
and the thought of smoking seaweed doesn't enter your head.

And while it's taken for granted everyone has relatives in Chicago
who share their grandmother's maiden name and seasonal lumbago,
it's probably worth remembering, at the risk of committing heresy,
as many families in Seatown have people in Blackpool and Jersey.

My own grandmother's uncle ran a Liverpool snooker hall
that cleaned up between the wars and went, of course, to the wall.
I must have a clatter of relatives there or thereabouts still
who have yet to trace their roots and with any luck never will.

I know there's a dubious aunt on my father's side in Blackburn,
a colony on my mother's in Bury called something like Bird or Horn.
I have a cousin a merchant seaman based in darkest St Ives,
another who came on in the seventies for Man. Utd. reserves.

If you're talking about inheritance, let me put it this way:
there's a house with umpteen bedrooms and a view of Dundalk Bay
that if I play it smoothly could be prefaced by the pronoun 'my'
when the old man decides to retire to that big after hours in the sky.

If it comes down to allegiance or a straight choice between
a trickle of shingly beaches that are slightly less than clean
and the rugged western coastline draped in visionary mystique,
give me the likes of Bray or Bettystown any day of the week.

If it's just a question of water and some half-baked notion
that the Irish mind is shaped by the passionate swell of the ocean,
I align myself to a dribble of sea that's unspectacular, or flat.
Anything else would be unthinkable. It's as simple as that.

Midweek

Take it for what it is:
a chance to lie low

outside the weekend's brackets,
to mark off time in minutes,

peat briquettes,
the cluster of units

a cursor eats up.
The sameness of distant bells

and a digital clock's ellipsis
and cars parked in a row

and the alarm waiting to trip
remains as good as intact —

apart from a dash to the line and back,
the night sky something else.

Come Again

You're set once more, and someone else
picks up her life above a shop
where you leave off. It never ends,
never changes. Friday is hope,
Sunday failure. Somewhere between,
all the words for returning drown
in the light of the same old scene
and rush-hour in a seaside town.

Given the time and space to care
what lies past any need for this,
given the length of days out there,
the yachts drifting on other skies,
it's unlikely you ever will —
although you couldn't ask for more
and evenings are brighter still
and you hold a key to her door.

Take then your leavetaking as read.
The future seems warm and lucky
beside this room, its couch-cum-bed,
your dog-eared *Farewell, My Lovely.*
Take it from now on that the road
and only thinking-the-world-of
and lately your weekending mode,
are more preferable than love.

How long will you carry it off?
Pretending to have gone too far
without going half far enough;
expecting no one to fall for
that smile and transitional air;
acting miles away and as though
whatever has been said to here
has escaped you from the word *Go.*

Green Baize Couplets

1
A handshake, a lowered light, the chance to clear her table
with what at first glance would appear to be a natural double.

2
Her colours on their spots, the cue-ball positioned perfectly . . .
Under normal circumstances, this would be a formality.

3
Still she rattles on. What I would give for a referee's voice
to bellow from the shadows an authoritative 'Quiet, please'.

4
A consummate technician, with one eye on the score,
intent on not over-reaching, keeping one foot on the floor.

5
Fallen beyond arm's length, I begin to feel the tension,
throw my eyes to heaven, and ask for the extension.

6
A sip of something on ice, having left it in the jaws,
to the horror of yours truly, the absence of applause.

7
After her kiss on the green, my unexpected cannon,
we go to the mid-session interval with honours pretty much even.

8
A hint of gentle side, a couple of messed-up plants,
a kick, a longish pink, and the glimpse of a second chance.

9
However long it takes, we'll continue this black ball fight
though by now the heat is off and the meter has run out.

10
Just as you join us, she has given me a shot to nothing,
and I am about to reply by pinning her to the cushion.

*

I know she knows I still believe
that when she tells him she loves him
there is an asterisk understood after 'love'
and a footnote qualifying her use of the term

for something which never quite measures up
like a storm on record but too long ago
or like an only international cap
in a friendly stopped by snow.

The Hall Light

An edge, a last chance among many others,
a halfway point in which to choose
to stand while outside January gathers
and your kitchen watches more bad news.

The hall light fills where nothing was
in adjoining rooms. It has been on
from four until this momentary pause
that falls between going and being gone.

A mile from now it will disappear
in a past tense where all day it snowed.
How far is Riverstown from here?
How far is Lordship from the road?

The television promises more bad weather
in the darkness behind our backs.
Putting the hall light out I dither.
I find little to say. I make tracks.

The Oral Tradition

You've heard it
  a million times before —
the one about
  ships in the night
where two perfect
  strangers find
that a few words
  and the air of a song
handed down from when
  the world was young
aren't all they share.
  So much so
it becomes increasingly
  hard to swallow.
It seems only proper
  to make off
in the opposite
  direction rather
than go along
  with the certainty
that one thing
  will naturally
lead to another.
  Then, after an age
hiking over miles
  of featureless land
in a dead heat,
  a receptionist
in a coastal town
  offers rolls and beer
after hours,
  bores you to tears
with stories of her
  mother and uncles
in the mountains,

and you think
that perhaps you
   should just toe
the line after all.
   She seems unsure
but undresses in your
   bathroom anyway
and cries for home
   when you kiss
a gradual ache
   between her legs.
Two men in the hall
   speaking double-dutch
and a squad car
   throwing violets on
the wall at dawn
   are all you'll recount
of the point when
   you in turn
come in her mouth.
   The following day
is the longest
   for many years.
She pays both fares
   on the bus inland
to where the trees
   and sun suddenly
are much higher
   and much warmer
than you can even
   begin to say.

The Sky Ceiling

by James Wyatt at Westport House in 1779

It could be dusk or dawn, whatever way one looks at it,
        or somewhere in between.
From now on only the gentleman and his man who of late
        have been and gone
can truly know whether callers unannounced will wait
        by the light of a sun
that forever is just about to rise or has just set.

Such is the fashion, to simplify the weather indoors
        to the gift or surprise
that a returning party journeys overnight towards
        under squalid skies
and on dawn's endless roads. Such are the rewards
        of overcoming adversities.
Such is the privilege a certain background affords.

To set aside one simply priceless spell from May
        to the very end of June,
when the height of summer has been punctuated only
        by a blade of moon
and by the picnic and flannels of an extended family
        afternooning on the lawn,
and press it between pages of tissue for a rainy day.

A day not unlike many in the midst of November's
        interminable drizzle.
Except that in anticipation of an absent master's
        descent from the capital
with old news, the household all morning prepares
        for the roll on gravel
that when it comes will take all expectation unawares.

And one who sits in the hall for what seems like hours
                   just for the pleasure
of leading another blindfolded through several doors
                   can be quite sure
that the canopy of blue and its far bands of cirrus
                   in the foreseeable future
won't darken to night and won't turn for the worse.

Ravenna

Someday, on a lark, I'll go to Ravenna.
I've thought for years of hiring a Lamborghini

and taking the eastbound route from Bologna
until towers are visible ten kilometres away.

I've heard that you can shut off the engine, get out,
and distinguish across the flat land a silhouette

of the city where Dante met his maker,
backed by yachts on the sea's lacquer.

I'll go in the wake of countless old stagers
who passed through its walls while various wars

blinked on the horizon; who saw how sweetness
gradually sours on its own excess,

and between them rebuilt a city from memory,
overshadowed by the past and a sugar refinery.

I'll go in late season and probably discover
that it's not much different from Portrush or Tramore.

The streets will be littered with chips, the façades
buried under the names of amusement arcades.

Saturdays will screech with gulls and bumper cars
and teenagers from the marshes cruising the wine bars.

Rock music will drone after hours and breakers
be floodlit by hordes of weekending bikers.

Someday I'll go to see the place itself
when the prospect of going is no longer enough.

Someday all this will be Ravenna:
a ring road glistening down to the marina;

a car parked at the shore; in the offing
another winter of canvas ruffling

and masts chiming; a foghorn which stammers
to an unreceptive shore; a red flag for swimmers

billowing its forecast for a gale at sea
to land in darkness and be greeted by me,

the token romantic who has driven
for three days on the trot to watch evening

shimmer on the Adriatic, who finds
a familiar gulf across which nothing shines.

Baltray

What day survives has yet to give, and may never.
The golf links ruffles a solitary number four.

The dunes are out of bounds, the grey lines gaining,
the lamp standards at the mouth of the estuary.

This is all by the way, all ancient history.
The word translates itself farther still from meaning

until the names for home and here are nothing more
than different tributaries of the same river.

Slip

and to know how to be Nobody,
like Ulysses, perhaps one needs the sea
　　　　　　— Claudio Magris,
　　　　　　　　　Danube

A path that holds
a thousand barnacles
and no definite end,

that's slowed at in passing,
even stopped at with
an hour or so to kill.

One of a handful
of dispersed survivors
from the Napoleonic wars,

touched up with cement
and with numbers frayed
to flecks of yellow paint.

A jaunt after dinner
is drawn to the blade
of soundless silver

by a feeling of being
able to walk at least
to the Isle of Man.

The scene of an artist's
impression of a storm
at sea that hangs

between the pool table
and the gents in a bar
twelve miles inland.

From there the road
loses its way through
cows and quaking grass,

passes a hotel-cum-shop,
a cluster of houses,
petrol pumps, a bus stop,

and keeps descending
until a whitewashed pillar
pushes into view.

It would appear
that everyone knows
there is nothing here

but legend and thin air
and a good prospect
of the Louth coast.

There are times when
November trades serenity
for a few rows of surf,

and visibility for
an opaque skyline,
a ship's whale-music.

There is talk
that young hoodlums
tinker with black magic

nearby on Saturday night.
The description of voices
and of a bobbing lamp

throws back to when
it was widely known
that some patriot,

at this very spot,
made his famous landing
or his famous flight.

A safe haven
in the days before
customs and automation,

for smuggling in the small
hours, for lightkeepers
clocking on and off.

Now only a gangplank
for terns and oystercatchers
and bewildered arctic waders,

a narrow slope
that's even overlooked
on the Ordnance Survey map.

Visible from a glider
as the point where
the sea's horses gather.

Glanced by the rotating
seasons, at intervals
by a migrating shadow,

and by the monotony
of light sliding over
and over like water.

Now stood on
only once or twice
in the calendar year.

When three out late
hear the waves are bad
on the front shore.

When one fits
some mackerel boxes
in the back of his Capri.

And when the odd
Sunday driver takes
a wrong turn on purpose

to make the spin last
half an hour longer,
drifts along side roads,

and happens on this
on the edge of nowhere,
bathed in sunshine.

There is no time
to dwell on metaphors
for an aimless life.

The town is far away.
The car doors
are left unlocked.

There is just long enough
to saunter down
in shirt sleeves,

spill some shingle from
one hand to the other
and wonder about the patch

of charred cans and ash,
the gulls scattering,
the pristine life-ring.

If the glazed window
piercing the haze
is dusk in Port Erin.

To whistle strands
of an unplaced air,
than call it a day.

Before the haze swells.
Before the tide
comes around again.

Acknowledgements and Notes

Acknowledgement is made to the editors of the following publications where many of these poems first appeared in various forms: *Ambit, Chapman, College Green, The Gettysburg Review, The Honest Ulsterman, The Independent, The Irish Review, The Irish Times, Krino, Lines Review, Metre, The New Republic, The North, Orbis, Oxford Poetry, P.N. Review, Poetry Ireland Review, The Rialto, The Steeple, The Sunday Times, Thumbscrew, TLS, Verse,* and *Westland Row.*

Selections appeared in *12 Bar Blues* (Raven Introductions) and *The Cloverdale Anthology.*

page 2:   "The Last Cage House in Drogheda"
            Cage house: Tudor style timber framed house. "Throughout Ireland wooden houses have now totally vanished though they were once numerous; indeed 16th century Dublin consisted mainly of cage-work houses. They suffered severely from the weather . . . and as they were seldom owner-occupied did not receive the regular maintenance they needed." *The Houses of Ireland,* by Brian de Breffny and Rosemary ffolliott, page 26. (Thames and Hudson, 1975).

page 32   "Progging"
            The title means to poke about, to hunt about for, *esp.* for food; to beg.

page 68   "∗"
            The first stanza adapts a sentence from Richard Ford's *Independence Day* (Harvill, 1995).

page 77   "Slip"
            'As if mirroring the duality of the old and new towns of Dundalk, of which it formed a part, Seatown had two names in the medieval period. As 'the Sea Town (*villa maryna*) of the Newtown of Dundalk,' it receives it first direct mention in the Anglo-Norman documentary sources

in 1372. . . . The second name, *Tráigh Baile,* in its variant form, 'Ballytra,' does not make an appearance in the same sources until the mid-sixteenth century.' Paul Gosling, *From Dún Delca to Dundalk. The topography and archaeology of a medieval frontier town* (1993).